A Gathered Distance

For the children

Published in 2020 by Birdfish Books
www.birdfishbooks.com.au

All rights reserved. No part of this edition
of this text may be reproduced or transmitted
in any form or by any means, electronic
or mechanical, including photocopy, recording
or any informational storage and retrieval system,
without prior permission from the publisher.

Cover images: *Sheoak with Female Flowers 1* (details), by Jacky Lowry
https://jackylowryartist.com.au/
and *Big Feather* (detail), by Meagan Brooker

ISBN-13: 978-0-9953718-4-2

A Gathered Distance

Poems

MARK TREDINNICK

2020

Acknowledgments

LIVING DISABLES us[1], sooner or later. This book records an instance. Among its other purposes—celebration, witness, seeing justice done, recasting life's exquisite spell, replenishment of language—lyric poetry, that deeper speaking, consoles like no other human accomplishment. Greg Orr[2] has argued that all cultures in all times have evolved the lyric poem to help humans, us languaging animals, survive spiritual catastrophe. Lyric poems do this by transfiguring inchoate and unbearable emotion into habitable places, intimate architectures of speech, gardens of language; a poem gives to airy nothings "a local habitation and a name."[3] Giving it a name and making it a place, a lyric poem can make of a grieving a hearth.

A poem puts your pain and delight back among the "family of things."[4] For a poem uses language connected to ecosystems of being and meaning and form and sense where one can feel whole, where one's sorrow has context, where one's solitude has company. And not merely social.

For each of us is all of us in a poem. The first person is only interesting in a poem, Seamus Heaney wrote somewhere, as an instance. An instance of being. A poem may cry pain, it may plead forgiveness, it may be a keening, a rant, an elegy, a refusal to go gently, a prayer. But the particulars of its witness are where it starts, not where it stops; each episode or image stands in a poem as a metaphor for all such moments—of anguish, sorrow, regret, desire, despair, gratitude, delight. A poem helps you find the myth in the moment, and so (as writer or reader) endure it. When profound human emotion can recruit the lyric, the personal can become the human, the particular the archetypal. And a collapse of self can become a gathering of distances, a habitat of healing.

It is my hope that a little of that goes on in *A Gathered Distance*. What poetry expresses is not one's self—or not merely. Poetry speaks all our selves.

In that sense, though they start with me, in a life like mine, in a disabling caused by living, these poems are not about me. This is not a memoir. These poems are the sense that poetry could help one human make of a great sadness, "that rust upon the soul," as Samuel Johnson puts it, that came his way with the end of a marriage and the fracture of a family. His disabling included grief and guilt and bewilderment and all the rest of it. In many ways these poems saved (and possibly improved) this poet. But if that's all they achieve, they are not the poems he hoped to write. For mine is just one instance of being, and it is one long moment of Being—in its exquisite multiplicity, in its contradictions and chaos and divine comedy—whose lyric I hoped to catch here, and in catching it make some sense, somehow, of the senselessness that Being sometimes seems to be.

To live is to move among the lives of others. And these poems wander others' lives a little. I write of others with what sounds, I hope, like the love I feel for those who've loved me and shared moments, days, whole long years, of this last era of my life; I write others as I write myself, as instances I've been blessed to know of human experience. Forgive me if I've fallen short. I thank my children, in particular, who are often mentioned here, for letting me speak of how some of these past years may have been for them, for us, and I apologise where I have failed to witness, though I have tried, the truth of things for them. Things are much better now for them and me, but there were hard times, and those times deserve this witness. Thank you to Anne and Sarah for seeing me through some of this, and for reminding me life is lyric even when it hurts. Thank you to my partner Jodie Williams with whom I've found joy; I know that poets are, among other things, hard to be with. Thank you to my elder children Michael and Louisa for standing steady through all this. Thank you to Brian Walters for your friendship, belief and support. Thanks, especially, to my friend Steve Armstrong for the wisdom and solid ground of your friendship, and for conversations in poetry that nurtured me and these poems. Thanks to other friends, including Don O, Michelle R, Michelle W, Debbie L, Roland, Kevin, Gerhardt, Peter Z, Colin M and Anne R. Others, too. I feel blessed in friends. Special thanks also to Tegan Gigante of Birdfish Books for taking on this book and making it a poem.

1. Thomas Szasz, in *The Myth of Mental Illness*, favoured "disabled by living" to "mental illness."
2. Gregory Orr, *Poetry as Survival*
3. William Shakespeare, *A Midsummer Night's Dream*
4. Mary Oliver, "Wild Swans"

SOME OF THESE POEMS have appeared, sometimes in different forms and under other titles, in journals and books. Some have won or shortlisted in prizes. Some were commissioned. I thank the editors and sponsors, publishers and judges for their support for my work and their permission to reprint the poems here.

"Pavane": *Almost Everything I Know*, Flying Island, 2014
"Father's Day (Or a Little After)": *Eureka Street*, No. 23, 2013
"Last Night I Went Out": *The Lyrebird*, Picaro 2010, Ginninderra 2017
"Little Lucy & the Tree": *Egret in a Ploughed Field*, The Chinese University of Hong Kong Press, 2018
"Desuetude": WRIT Poetry Review, No 1, 2014
"Nightfishing": Ron Pretty Poetry Prize 2014 (Shortlist)
"End of a Lonely Day": ACU Poetry Prize 2016 (Shortlist)
"The Horse": ACU Poetry Prize 2016 (Winner); *The Lyrebird*, 2017; *Egret in a Ploughed Field*, 2018
"Icarus": *Eureka Street*, No.23 2013; *Poem & Dish*, 2014
"Daedalus at Midlife": *Metamorphic*, Recent Works, 2017
"A Gathered Distance": commissioned by Red Room Poetry, written on my residency at Sydney Botanic Gardens, 2017; published in *New Shoots Poetry Anthology*, Red Room Poetry, 2017. (You can read part of the poem on a plaque in the gardens.)
"The Habit of Wings": *AXON* C1, 2016; *Best Australian Poems* 2016
"The River Running Shallow": Newcastle Poetry Prize 2018 (Second)
"Grief Wears a Body": Newcastle Poetry Prize 2018 (Longlist)
"Tomorrow": written for the Bendigo Botanic Gardens as creative in residence at landscape architecture firm TCL; published in *Anthology: An Essay in Plants, Poetry & Image*, TCL, 2017
"The Blue Pasture": ACU Poetry Prize 2019 (Shortlist)
"Picton Morning; Picton Afternoon": *St Mark's Review*, Issue 238, December 2016
"Along the Road": *Sijo: An International Journal of Poetry and Song*, Seoul, 2018
"First Light": *The Lyrebird*, 2017

"Grace, and a Barking Owl": Newcastle Poetry Prize 2019 (Longlist)
"A Forest Inside": *St Mark's Review*, Issue 238, December 2016
"The Fire & the River & the City & the Bush": commissioned by Red Room Poetry and published December 2019 in their Fellowship Shortlist anthology.
"Egret in a Ploughed Field": *Egret in a Ploughed Field*, Chinese University of Hong Kong, 2017

(Image: Oliver Damian)

MARK TREDINNICK—the author of *The Little Red Writing Book*, *The Little Black Book of Business Writing*, *Almost Everything I Know*, *Fire Diary*, *The Blue Plateau*, and a dozen other works of poetry and prose—is a celebrated poet, essayist, and writing teacher. His bestselling books on the writing craft are used in schools and university writing programs and have inspired a generation of writers. His many honours include the Montreal and Cardiff Poetry Prizes, The Blake, ACU, Ron Pretty, and Newcastle Poetry Prizes, two Premiers' Literature Awards, and the Calibre Essay Prize. *The Blue Plateau*, his landscape memoir, shortlisted for the Prime Minister's Prize. Sir Andrew Motion has said of Mark's work:

"His is a bold, big-thinking poetry, in which ancient themes (especially the theme of our human relationship with landscape) are recast and rekindled."

In addition to *A Gathered Distance*, two new collections of poetry, *Walking Underwater* and *The Beginner's Guide* appear in 2020, and Mark is at work on *Reading Slowly at the End of Time*, a memoir of a reading life.

In 2018, Mark was writer in residence at the University of Sydney; and he was a guest of the Berlin Literature Festival, and the Xichang Qionghai Silk Road International Poetry Week. In April 2109 he was a guest of the International Writers' Program at the Lu Xun Literature Academy in Beijing; in November 2019, he was a guest of the Miluo International Poetry Festival.

Mark travels and teaches widely, in schools and at festivals, and he works with the corporate sector as a mentor, speaker and copywriter. The father of five, he lives with his partner Jodie Williams on the Wingecarribee, southwest of Sydney. He teaches poetry and rhetoric at Sydney University and the University of Technology, Sydney.

Contents

Prologue

Early Summer Sijo   3

I—Pavane

Pavane   7
Father's Day (Or a Little After)   8
Nocturne   10
Frost   12
Wreck   13
Last Night I Went Out   14
A Kind of Dying   15
Little Lucy & the Tree   16
Desuetude   17

II—On Dusk

Nightfishing   21
Upended Landscape   22
End of a Lonely Day   23
The Horse   24
Icarus   27
Daedalus at Midlife   29
A Gathered Distance   32
The Habit of Wings   37
Down by the Reservoir on Dusk   39

III—Four Rooms

Oblivion	43
Running into my Youth	44
The River Running Shallow	45
Cloud Shadow	50
Grief Wears a Body	51
Four Rooms	53
The Kiss	55
Tomorrow	57
A Morning	59
Grief's Work	64
The Blue Pasture	65
Two Boys	66
Three Poems	67
Kite & Cumulus	68
Come, Play	70
What the Light Tells	72
Picton Morning; Picton Afternoon	73
My Children Are in My House	76
Passing Picton	78
Along the Road	85
Between	86

IV—First Light

First Cold Night	91
Slime Rhymes	93
Back When	94
Picton Clouds	96
A Boy, One Afternoon	99
On Bowral Station, Waiting for the Early Train, One July Morning	101
The Leaves	102
First Light	103
A Star Fell Last Night	104
A Small Poem for Spring	106
Grace, And a Barking Owl	107
Talking Death Down	109
A Forest Inside	110
A Scattering	111
The Fire & the River & the City & the Bush	113
Yesterday's Poem	116

Epilogue

Egret in a Ploughed Field	121

Notes   125

Prologue

Early Summer Sijo

STILL WATER in a glass: the invisible world finds a form.
   I drink and taste emptiness,   a flavour older than the sun.
Cicadas cry ten years underground   into three days on earth.

I

Pavane

Pavane

I thought it said on the girl's red purse
A kind of sad dance and all day
wondered what was being defined…
The real love that follows
early delight and ignorance.
A wonderful sad dance that comes after.

—Jack Gilbert, "Pavane"

I MAY BE sitting inside the best afternoon
The world has put on since the Permian
Extinction.
          Except for the solicitous
  Passage of a few cars, like the last birds,
Along the road out front, you might think
  The world had stopped breathing.
                            Until
The kookaburras start up like a brass band
  Out of practice, and the children's voices
Tumble from the house like applause.
  The wind picks up a stitch in time and
Drops it in the amber elms.
                    From the pear trees
  That stand at my study window, fruit hang heavy
In the harvested light.
                 And the afternoon is a blue
  Pavane, dancing gravely by in geologic time,
Her eyes closed, her lips parted, and her mouth
  Full of catastrophic promises.

Father's Day (Or a Little After)

SHE SAID I was fifty-two and weighed sixty-eight kilograms
    And stood one-and-a-half metres tall, and some of that
Is right.
      She said my hair was brown and that my beard was grey
  And prickled when I kissed her, which she said was often.
                                                                        She said
I was good at writing and drawing and soccer and not so good
   At cooking. He likes to ride horses, she said (though she never
Saw me). He draws me birds.
                              She said if I were a superhero,
  I'd be Superman, and she didn't say why. She loved me,
She said, because I hugged her all the time (but who could not?)
   And because I was funny.
                                 She emphasized that. Then, smaller:
"He is busy **a lot**!" But he reads to me and he listens when
   I read to him. He loves Mr Todd,
                                        and I love Timmy Tiptoes.
But she was sick when Father's Day came, and she forgot
   To give me the sheets where she wrote all this in class.
She gave them to me today and didn't want to talk about it
   When I got out of the car to catch the train again.
                                                        He buys me
Toys from Sydney, she had written—as if toys were spices
   And Sydney were Tashkent. Later, when she called to say
Goodbye properly on her mother's phone, she couldn't get the
   Words out. And oh, there is no pain so pretty as how well

PAVANE

A young girl likes to miss her dad.
                                No heart so easily wronged—
   Or righted again—as hers. Nor any heart so far gone
                For good quite so often as his.

Nocturne

I DON'T LIKE to wonder too long
   What it says about me that I
       Love my loved ones best asleep.
      Tonight, then, is a photograph
Of the good life, prettily framed: love
   Asleep in three beds at once, in five
       Or six abandoned poses, and I sit
      At a desk afloat in a callow light,
Which leaks from two lamps, one
   Each side of the bed, and swills
       Against the windows and the darkness
      Their glass is cut from. Debussy's fingers
Are all over the radio, and the rain falls
   Fat and sporadic on the roof. A small frog
       Is splayed across one windowpane, casing
      The joint indiscreetly, caught short
In an awkward rappel, and the dog
   Is at the window now, wanting a piece
       Or two of the moth that's trying to steal
      The light that just will not escape the night
Blindness of the bedroom's gaze. And
   Behind me on cotton sheets that map
       In three dimensions the geomorphology
      Of a young girl's refusal to go quietly

PAVANE

Into a father's nocturne, my daughter
    Breathes a heavy syncopation in her
        Sleep and turns and turns as if to shake
      Me from some fractious, ancient idyll
Afoot in her sleepy head.

Frost

Woke up this morning with
a terrific urge to lie in bed all day
and read. Fought against it for a minute.

Would I live my life over again?
Make the same unforgiveable mistakes?
Yes, given half a chance. Yes.

—Raymond Carver, "Rain"

I WAKE EARLY into a morning that's lying in late
   All over a view I can barely see through a frost
That's made the windows over into mysteries.

The coldest morning of the year, I'd guess, and no wind
   Anywhere. My soul's the winter solstice, and where
The tap drips down the back, a six-inch icicle hangs

Like time's arrow paused in its falling, and the trough
   Is an ice rink for rose robins. The grass is brittle
Under my boots, and already I'm looking back on a life

Held fast inside a winter moment, and seeing most of what
   Escaped me (while I lived it): How I loved and how
I was loved and how like rivers all the limpid shadows run.

Wreck

THE MOON IS yellow and the night is black—
   The usual deal, struck by nine and written out
Longhand by the winter trees across the winter

Sky. The frogs are back. The same old world
   He left behind, and someone like the man he used to be
Before he was, you know, so exquisitely unmade

By the full moon, and you, walks out into the night and
   Tries to recollect himself. This used to be so easy; it used
To seem so real. No map now but the memory of your skin.

Last Night I Went Out

AND SAT cross-legged on the road
    And smoked a cigarette on the centreline.
Don't ask me why.
              It was well after one
  And nothing was likely to come along,
And nothing did.
              You, for instance.

A Kind of Dying

I MOW ALL morning long and after
Noon I split the afternoon in two (and three and four…)
To fuel the winter count of coming night. I chase
My dog's delight all day,
While winter steeps everything in everything else and holds it very dear; I swim
The tide of light out, and I swim it back in; and then what
Can a father do, I think, but throw
All his hope wide like a net
Beneath the pear tree, into whose high crown a daughter climbs at dusk
To pull the night down like a curtain.
The world returns,

From nowhere, thus, to convince me
I'm alive; but life is nowhere near enough. It's a kind of dying
I want: to recollect my self, to be
Of any use to anyone.
There's a second life deep within—and all around—my days; there are clothes
That used to fit. They lay me out and try me on and make me
Try again. They pick up my pen and write
The world less thin. They come like
Bowerbirds, like rose robin and Facebook posts and children
Fast asleep; they settle like solitude
And a good slow fire,
And all eternity to burn.

Little Lucy & the Tree

S HE NEVER SAW a tree she didn't need
                                        to climb. Some things you have to see
Can only find you there. She needs loft, my girl.
Limbs. A father's arms will do, but nothing beats
A tree. A birch, she's learned, will leave the distance
(Where it is) and make a garden grow
                                  a sky. A decade old

Today, a digit for each syllable
                              of her name; still
In the lower branches of her years,
But already taller than her days, she's bright
With all the light she learns up there.
                                      I think of how I couldn't find her
On the day I had to leave. At last, I heard her amber voice

Fall down from high up
                      where she leafed out
In the poplar's crown. *I'm teaching the tree to see*, she said.
And, ah, you are the summer
                              of my grief, my girl, as near to heaven
As I would ever hope to reach.
You teach my days to hope again. You coach
                                    my forest heart to yield.

Desuetude

IT RAINED FOR weeks when you left, and it's rained all night
  Tonight, and the morning's so suddenly bright that
The windows weep, taking the morning in.
                                       The heart carries on
  Like children's play, long after someone's mother's called
Time and already the dusk is deep and all the light is lost.
  Love goes on years after love's stopped working.
                                               Down the back,
For instance, a tractor lies rusting in the field, and there's
  A ghost at the wheel, and it's learning very slowly how to
Stop: it's taking lessons in the weather, sitting late with the night
  Herons, failing like the grasses to stay green, and refusing like
The larches to let go of the lake.
                                A marriage ends; a family lasts;
  Love has nowhere else to stay. But here. Until, at last, the tractor
Is the field again, and the ghost becomes the genius of the place.
  And rain starts up and falls on down,
                           for all it knows is falling
                                               to the ground.

II

On Dusk

Nightfishing; or On Dusk

ON DUSK tonight, I drove down through sandstone
    Onto the bridge at Mooney Mooney, and above
The Hawkesbury, wide at that point, a crescent
   Moon, its second night out, tossed in shallows.
            It's possible to sit as still as stone at 120 kph,
And that's what I did as I looked up at the moon, and
   It seemed to me a small boat bobbing there in that
Estuary, the night; and I let myself imagine its cargo
   As my three young children, whom I cannot see just
Now, and whose voices are like birds at night. It was
   A sentimental thought, I know,
            brought on by tiredness and journeying
And the coming down of night, but it drew them close,
   Those three, when they cannot be.
                          It buoyed me to find them
   Out so late, rowing that bright barque in the dark above me,
Here in country I feel cut from like timber, and I let my mind
   Swim to them, those small fishers,
                      casting for me in shallows.

Upended Landscape

HEAVY SKY like upended foothills
                    under snow, traps beneath it (or is it above?)
A white mid-morning light, that slides in off the sea. My
Life has fallen from its axis;
                          it kilters this way and that, a buoy

That tosses on the tide. I've lived
                          too much in thought, perhaps,
Standing on my head these fifty years. I want a body to
Fall into now: two legs to walk me
                          out of here,
                                    a mouth to breathe *Amen*.

End of a Lonely Day

END OF A lonely day
    Spent watching rain
  Showers lift and fall,
Drafting—and erasing—landscapes
                        across the hours.
  My children are scattered like thoughts
I could not keep.
        Night falls
  On the harbour now, and I search
For a book to keep me
  From my grief,

        to find my sorrow—
  And recollect my wealth—written
Out in other lives and other times and ways:

    For each of us is all of us,
                in the end, and morning
Is only hours away.

The Horse

Real drawing is a constant question,
is a clumsiness, which is a form
of hospitality towards what
is being drawn.

—John Berger, *Portraits*

there is a landscape, veined, which only a child can see
or the child's older self, a poet…

—Adrienne Rich, "Dreamwood"

SHE'S AT A LOSS, my daughter, in the drawing
   She makes, a girl and her horse, as a gift
For me—a frontispiece she pens,
   Beside my name, which she inscribes
As if it were her own, on the first page
   Of my new notebook:
                       Freckles and a quandary
Upon her face; one foot in one camp,
   The other in another. Her face asks
A question to which her body wants
   An answer.
             And beside her, a horse, and
It leans her way, the way she's drawn it,
   This pony, infinitely tender, waiting for her,
The girl in the picture, to notice that she,

The girl with the pen, already has
What she always wanted, standing
   At her side.
                     When I lived with her, she rode
Me sometimes; sometimes, though she's nine,
   And is beginning to forget, she rides me still.
I have loved horses and ridden them, and
   Every birthday and Christmas, knowing
Her hope was hopeless, she's asked for one,
   Which never came.
                     We've loved horses together,
She and I, and her hope for horses was our
   Love for each other, and I drew them
For her from The World of the Horse,
   And from storybooks I gave her because
I couldn't give her a horse.
                     We loved each other
   Many ways, but how we both loved horses
Was how we loved each other best.
                     If I tell you,
   Then, we are the horse she's drawn, she and I,
Or that I am the horse and she is the girl,
   You'll know why, and you'll understand
How her drawing cries my longing
   For her, the way it sings her longing
For us.
          Opening my journal, tonight, I see
   The two of us, hopeful and kind and confused,
Wondering how we stand now and what
   Will become of all we loved, and what will
Become of us.

              Knowing, as children
  Know—and drawings that are real—much
More than she knows, my girl has drawn
    A question to which I—to which we—are
The answer in the horse's eye: *Yes*, I want
    To tell her; *yes*.
                    What you long for, my love,
Stands beside you, a father beside his girl,
    All you ever wanted, a horse that will not
Run, an answer more tender than time.
                                What you long
    For longs for you, and even when you
Cannot see me, and you are not sure
    I know, I know.
                    I stand beside you, my girl,
And I stood there all along, and I stand
    Beside you ready, all the days of your life.

Icarus

Everyone forgets that Icarus also flew.

—Jack Gilbert, "Failing and Flying"

LIKE SOME nocturnal Icarus,
I dream too close to heaven—
         I fly too close to morning—
and I wake in pieces. And so
         I woke this Wednesday, a child
disarmed in sleep and felled
         By the gravity of the ancient light
he dawns in. But I rose—
         A trick Icarus mastered just once,
but oh how he mastered it! —
         And I walked straight out into
everything, feeling too poor
         For the wealth of my days,
and wondering what became
         Of the currents that buoyed me
yesterday. Driving to work,
         Regretting the towers that grow
now where horses
         Used to run, I passed on the road
a felled bird: An Indian
         Mynah, pariah of the suburbs,
freshly dead and stuck for good now

　　　　　　In the slow lane. A circle of his kind
stood a brown mourning around him.
　　　　　　　Making sure; ministering his passage.
One moved forward to check
　　　　　　His pockets; the others, though,
held back, piecing together
　　　　　　　A memory of how he flew.

Daedalus at Midlife

For Philip Gross

A LIGHT RAIN has come
                         in the night like sleep—a better
   Sleep, a softer fall, a kinder kind of waking

Than I have known in years. My body lies and longs
   For rest my mind won't let me keep. A grief two decades

Deep is all I know each dawn. I lie and implore
   Sleep to hold a while yet and steep me whole

Again, and, when it won't, and won't again, I cry:
   I'm done with life. With living on, if sad is all,

Or most of all, a man can be. If anguish—gone
   Last night—is going to break each day, then give me death,

At least for now, until this agony has spent
   Itself upon itself, and laid waste time, and passed:

I'll come back then.
                     I rise instead into a clearing
   Sky and as the light unspools like thread and spreads,

And wrens reprise again their "Blue in Green", the rain
   Begins again. It falls as sound, a peaceful piece,

A steady riff, my mind—unmanned by this too much
    To bear, and lost in work my heart should rather do—

Would like my coming days to learn. I'm called, I know,
    To fashion a life, without the tools I used to use

To shape one. Somewhere here I have them; I set them down,
    When life and work—which until then had seemed so much

Like play, and earth the envy of heaven—fell down and drowned
    The only child I used to be, and orphaned me,

His father. If only the dark would throw some light and help me,
    Blind, to find them. But this is an old man's plaint;

I'm exiled from myself.
                      And through my craft I've made
    Of all that's left of life a labyrinth I'm lost in.

Under the hands of the masseur today—who divined in my back,
    Bent too long at the work of my mind, reservoirs

Of sorrow deep as seas and older yet than tides—
    I began to drop into the body of my grief.

The world is made of metamorphoses: each day
    Becomes the next.
                    And I'd become myself again,

ON DUSK

If there were gods who'd hear a prayer these days and nod.
    But no, it wouldn't be the life I had, my mind

Too bright with wings that flew too high and far. This ageing
    Life, this father self, is all that I'd become.

To grow my mind some legs
                        and walk it back into
    The way things are: the brokenness, the rain that falls.

A Gathered Distance

ACROSS the harbour's fetch,
                    a distance grows, a loveliness
  Of limbs. By night the gardens are everything
A city's not, a sleep it never takes, a dream of antique mornings

Run to seed. The gardens on the cove might
                    almost be one's other life. A silence
  Adumbrated, where wisdom takes its time
To grow, and all the many selves you are assemble in the dark

And in the morning resemble
                    a coagulated distance where freedom
  Holds, a love lost, a child found, a sadness almost bearable.
Another way. Upon beguiled sandstones, in swamps made almost good,

Other times and other natures
                    have put down roots and in a hundred languages
  Refute the simpler thoughts our minds would rather think
About the nature of a place. The middle of the year

Blew in last night and talk of
                        winter wandered up the coast
  From the deep Antarctic south, and Saturday morning paints
An absence wide enough to welcome every thought

It cares to keep. From here I see a mythic plinth,
                        a folly, proudly out of place, and far,
  Like all of us, from home; I see a palm and hear the surf
It stood by; I see a mob of figs, ebullient and overweight,

Strangers swallowing their hosts,
                        murderers become a forest on remand.
  And I see hoop pines, those geomancers, slow-motion dancers,
Sadly out of step with trippy times like these,

Extending their courtly hands
                        to gather up the light, to catch the news
  Feed, the current account of things, and from it piece together
A past. And in among the burnished canopies,

The noble green pavilions, where all
                        the elsewheres in the world make camp,
  I see the swamp oaks rise like smooks,
The frail exhalations of four or five fires refusing even yet

To go out. The gardens make
                       a thousand distances
   A shapely thicket of repose. A stubborn stillness holds there,
A recursive gladness in which all sadness also inheres,

Leafs out and fruits the future
                       as if it didn't give a damn.
   And notwithstanding the savage rush of things, a simplicity holds
The hands of time a while here, remembers

And calls you *child*. Offers you
                       stories and, under the stories' breath,
   Leaves like archipelagos, flowers like feckless continents adrift,
And each day death forgets its dance steps and lives on another day.

How a garden hangs together—this one
                       an instance, like the rest of us, of all of us—is how
   One might cohere and carry on. A garden is never
Finished, and nor are you: Become, I think, a garden again,

And never, like a garden, cease; find
                       in every bed and nest, and step out along
   Each pathway, and read in every leaf, more elliptical renderings, daily,
Of the oracle of your life: how to live it as you fathom it

By loving what is worthy of your love.
                Find in every episode
  Of weather, in every sudden gladness a garden gives and takes,
In every child that comes, in every fallen feather of each itinerant

Bird; find in the circular migration
                      of the eels, in the invaginated flowering
  Of the fig, in the stubborn insistence of things,
In beauty's refusal not to be—find a way to continue

To thrive, to flourish even, if you can,
                regardless, to set seed, even when hope
  Has lost its flight feathers and strangeness
Has swallowed the way your life ran, and your days

Have run off sideways and become a week
                of showers. Be a garden in a city,
  And be all the love you've lost. From all the unpropitious
Pieces tending toward a self, cultivate a solitude, harvest half

A life and make it whole. Gather all your distances, and
                father all your orphan fears; hold them
  Near, as a father might, his children scattered now,
If only he could. Husband all the futures up from out of all the pasts.

And make a garden
                       of every sorrow you never will
  Outgrow. Plant every single thing you never really understood,
And watch it become a tree, and stand under it, and know why.

The Habit of Wings

Your grief for what you've lost lifts a mirror
up to where you are bravely working.

Expecting the worst, you look, and instead,
here's the joyful face you've been wanting to see.

Your deepest presence is in every small contracting and expanding,
the two as beautifully balanced and coordinated
as birdwings.

—Rumi, "Birdwings"

EVERY SEASON is more than itself alone;
    Each moment and slow passage of time

Has a twin. Feeling bleak and daunted
    All this grey Easter long—doing grief's

Work, as it's best done, alone—I caught
    In the mirror, more than once, a man

So much lighter than the man I'd been
    Hauling about, like a burlap sack

Of granite, like four decades of dropped
    Anchors, and he put me in mind, this other

Self, of a goshawk making ready for flight.
    And for a moment, that's stretched

Into a week, I flew, too (thankful for
    The mirror and the doubleness of things).

Sometimes one's flown the cage, already,
    That holds one in. One heals by bearing

The pain and all the days one's left behind;
    One heals by setting them aside. Inside

The stone, there's light; inside the heft
    And harrow of all you've lost, a flight

That aches for air. The soul wants,
    First, to clench and then to spread its

Fingers. Love is made of feathers and of
    Bone—and healing has the habit of wings.

Down by the Reservoir on Dusk

For Lindsay Tuggle

1.

DOWN BY the reservoir on dusk the dwindled light
   Leaves white the only colour standing
And returns to ghost gums bodies they depart
   By day.
        The gathered waters shine, too,
As if they were a hearth for starlight.
                        I walk
   The shores late to take the steps I let
The day steal from me, sitting at my desk.

2.

   It's hard to make out in this ebb if what
Resembles wasted breath expelled like smoke
   Along the water's surface is a rising
Fog, or if it's space the crickets' chorus
   Makes, inside the falling dark, for all
That day occludes.
               And walking here I find
   Again the rest of who I am among
The throng of all that isn't mine to mend.

III

Four Rooms

Oblivion

For Kevin Young

I WAKE as if I knew the news had broken bad
   Already.
         The peace I rest in overnight retreats
As daylight starts its engine on a Stanmore Street.

  I want oblivion, my lord; this living on
Is hard.
      But no, let's give this one more go, I say
  And walk outside to smoke. The morning is a better

Man than this one I've become, the sun a bene-
   Faction wasted on a terraced street;
                           the early
August light is all the years to come. There is

  A life that wants to walk me worthy of how much
It's cost.
     Oblivion can wait till sunlight can't
  Remember how to fall, and I've no body left

For it to find, no habits left to break. And when
   The news comes in,
                it is already old; the future's
Here to hold it, and my mind to let it go.

Running into My Youth

For Steve Armstrong

I LEFT MY RUN late, day failing fast, the moon so new it hurt
   To remember when the whole world lay ahead of you like that.
It bore the coming dark, though, like an orb, and showed me I might,

Too. As I ran the two Ks out, each leg felt all its fifty-
   Something years: a century bore me, unsteadily at first,
Between the sheoaks and the oaks, the blue pastures and the 'burbs,

But the track knew its way, and I let it lead. Starlings started.
   Kingfishers settled into lodgings made fast by song. I swerved
Around a peak-hour snarl of dogs; I found phrases on the fly

To greet families, like the one I used to have, walking down
   The curtain on the day. I shared my *low moan* with the heifer
Pulling up bunch grass by the fence. The breast of Razorback ridge

Rose in two or three hundred million years of sleep and stars birthed
   In the breath it held, and, when I reached the halfway hedge and turned,
It occurred to me I'd forgotten myself, slipped from my mind's

Firm grip. And making for home in the full dark, the moon now sailed
   Past seeing, my life became a lighter thing to bear, my years
Dropped overboard like ballast, grief's anchor weighed and love's lines cast.

I set out so old I almost did not start at all; I reached
   The beginning young, begun again. And hope's a gift you earn
By following your feet, by letting your place remember you.

The River Running Shallow

1.

NOTHING THE WORLD was once so gifted at
    Knows how to fill the silence that my children
Leave, gone missing from my days.
                                      Give
  Yourself back to what you love, they say,
But all I give the sadness takes away. I try
  To muscle up, building a body fit to bear
All that my mind cannot. My arms grow
  Strong, my stomach taut, but who is there
Anywhere to hold and swing and play the fool
  And lift high in the surf?
                                  I try to love again,
But something in me cannot learn to yield
  To love's insubordinate commands, and all delight's
Become a foreign currency that buys me
  Nothing here.
                  I used to learn fast, and I know
It's myself I need to study to understand,
  My own life, and what's inherent there
And adequate and entire. I score well at
  The multi-choice of the examined life,
But when they want an essay, all that comes
  To mind is every day I live a half-life
In the absence of my children's names.

2.

    DUSK along the river knows nothing
About three children who never, so far, walked it
    With me; the river running shallow way
Down deep in its four-storeyed banks is innocent
    Of all three storeys of the house my mind
Bears on its back: my grief for the living,
    Taught each day I'm dead to them, for days
I used to know with them, days died back
    Like forest after fire on which the rain
Disdains to fall;
              the violence done to hope
    Each day it wakes in them and rises in me
And tries to fly us back together again;
    And down in the basement, the deep despair that floods
The circuitry that used to keep the lights on
    Day and night, the chaos that corrodes
The chemistry the mind employed to make
    Each minute mean a world.
                        I've lost the rhythm,
Misplaced the algorithm, that used to know
    My way. But here outside myself, it seems,
A universe is being born, a place
    That wants me in it.

3.

                    ITS INNOCENCE of me
And mine is what I take myself to the river
   To find, when the heat of unrelenting days
Of summer begins to yield at dusk: the silence
   The sheoaks and the bracken have no mind
To keep, the patience the creek's the master of
   (The way it is, no matter what things seem),
The truth that is the only thing that it knows
   How to tell. The river at dusk can keep
My cries and teach my feet and both my thighs
   To carry me on until my silence one day
Spills again its banks.
                  Till then, the river
   Is my Orpheus and I, its underworld.

4.

AND by the fence the cattle crop the grass,
   And in a rising easterly the sheoaks
Sing all distance into one lament,
   And a wagtail raps a sweet farewell.
                                 The wilding
Weather wants the blue shirt off my back,
   And a whipbird, the sweetest dominatrix in
The world, sings her lash and elicits a cry,
   A happy lullaby from her helpless, hapless
Mate. A working man walking calm
   His working dog catches me, taking illicit
Pictures of the sky, and I walk with him
   A mile and talk and find myself a man
Again, any other per-ambulant tenant
   Of a place, a being on the earth.

5.

AND at the bend a foretaste of the evening
   Pools and wells, and I swim the scent of ages
Past, the learning way down deep in things,
   And I feel a coolness like the dawn upon
My skin.
        The sky, meantime, premeditates
   Some rain, which, as I turn, deigns to fall,
Desultory, a while, upon the descent
   Chat of children after dinner, beyond
The hedge.
         And step by step my mind relents,
   And night becomes a house where all I carry
Puts itself to bed—three children, tired
   Now of being every sound that heard them
In my head, and every way they were not
   Here, but were the rehabilitated
Sense the river running shallow in deep
   Banks made of where I found myself,
Accompanied each step by all I love.
   Before they sleep my children read me this:
Grief is proof of love; it lets you walk
   "The sweet music of your particular heart"
In step with all you thought you'd lost—but can't.

Cloud Shadow

CLOUD SHADOW makes a forest of the hill;
   Above, fair-weather cumulus flare in blue
Wastelands, the only thoughts the morning mind
   Of autumn cares to think.
                      Through which I run,

Moving my limbs to teach my mind to still,
   Racing the river across the bridge in hope
My mood might rise and take the bait the sunlight
   Casts upon the day.
                      Fruitbats in figtrees

Festive in sleep, laugh at my enterprise;
   Trouble begins to seep from me like sweat.
Home again and spent, I sit on the deck
   And let my body catch my breath,
                      and think:

My mind's a thousand years of overcast
   And plot and speed and anguish,
                      but just look:
The day is nothing but the present tense;
   All darkness has its counterpoint in light.

Grief Wears a Body

GRIEF WEARS a body,
                         and today she stands in mine.
   The rose bush by my stoop, flush with blooms that flared
In seven long unearthly days of heat,
                               bends at daybreak toward the east,
  Beneath a night of heavy rain. Nothing readies you
For when it wants to leave. You learn to grieve
                                     by grieving, and nothing must rush the work.

Rain will fell you earthward;
                         be in no haste to rise. Grief lasts as long
   As love was deep. Mourning is work that chooses you
Exactly when you want it least.
                             I want to say it's work that doesn't pay,
  But there's a living you earn by putting in the time.
Grief pays for what it takes by all it gives.
                         Is grieving the living

The hardest grief to learn,
                 the most like death, itself?
   You know my story now: three children I used to live with live
With me now in pictures
                 I've posted on my wall. And how I miss
   Them only my body knows: my left hip is where
My daughter lives, and how it aches at dawn.
                             I bend, like the rose

A GATHERED DISTANCE

In prayer that weighs me down,
                                       and there she is in how I let her go.
  My elder boy inhabits my right arm,
A bicep I work too hard at weights I lift
    To give back to my body the waiting work
                                      my mind's too fast to do. And where
Is my middle boy? That lion lives in my toes,
                               numb with age and boots I wore

That never really fit.
                This is the alchemy of sorrow, that *rust*
  Upon the soul: to teach you how to dwell in what you've lost, and it
To dwell in you, making absence over into presence more profound.
    Grief is a body that only knows how
                            to heal by how it hurts. Until it doesn't so much
Anymore. I tie the rose. My children prick
                        my finger there and laugh,
                                          and all the weather clears.

Four Rooms

For Jodie Williams

1.

SORROW's a room I keep for my children. I sweep it
   Clear of leaves; weather litters it and I sweep it
                  clear again. I burn a lamp there, for the room
Is dark, and I want it bright for them.
                              My house has other rooms—my life is larger
  Than the days and voices missing from it. A father's heart's a biome; his mind, a moiety.
All this is wealth, I say, and one day I'll be rich enough to believe it.
                  One's life's a gift it's right to earn by giving back.
                          Waiting alone won't buy you the credit you need.

2.

I WAKE in Xichang between a mountain and a lake.
   All the years the mountains carry
                    here, the time they took to dawn and forest
Their flanks and start to forget themselves again—all these well at Langshan's feet
                         in waters that want to be a sea one day: Qionghai.
  Swallows wander lay-lines in the early mist. Spring, they tell you, winters here all year.
And fir trees walk a prayer upon the shores. Peacocks woke us yesterday; today it's grief—
                convinced that all the birds have squandered all the song;
                      sure this time that daylight's got the colours wrong.

3.

WHERE WAS IT, dear, you learned, in all the years
    Before you knew my skin, the knack
                        of bringing up my bones? Old poets say that wine
Is good for grief; I find weeping best. What the soul can no more name
                        than bear, the body must find a song for. And so,
    Mine does, until what's broken in the world is almost pieced together in my bed.
I open a window and climb through.
                        The morning is cool and steeped in the scent of pines.

4.

THE MOUNTAIN is tall with autumn and old with spring.
    The birds who've kept their peace
                        these three still days become a chorus now, a kindergarten
Choir, reciting all the joy and woe this land has known,
                        and we are here to join awhile.
    Terns take turns in lazy cadence on the lake. Grebes dive shallow waters low
With drought and scavenge seagrass meadows,
                        which grow like weeds where all one's sorrows sleep.

The Kiss

For Russell

MY BROTHER held me the other day,
    Saying farewell, and kissed me.
                          This was at his school,
   Where he's a senior man, and it was early
Fall, and the sun slept in the sky like a cat
   On a couch, and I was a visiting fellow.
                                  My life
Must have looked, in other eyes than his, already
   A job well-done.

Down all the years we never kissed:
   That's not what our family did, and I wished
In that moment it had.
                   If you cannot
   Feel loved in a brother's arms, something is badly
Awry. And something was.
                     In the rasp of our faces,
   Though, one against the other, and a breeze
Picking up from the east, and the first magpie larks
   Of the midyear beginning their broken-down song, two
Half-lives lived estranged in one blood congealed
   And a dozen old wounds healed.

                      And what was wrong
In me, and what is wrong in all of us,
    And in the forsaken world, came right; and as I
Walked to my car in the sun, a loneliness fifty-
    Five years deep seemed to begin to fall,
              Like ice, in a warming world, away.

Tomorrow

For Peter Zawal

THE FUTURE is hard
            to know. Tomorrow is an act
   Of faith. The way ahead is blind; the way back closed.
Each day is a stranger, a beggar,
                        a god. More will be wanted

Of you than you think you know
                how to give. But if you welcome
   Each moment that finds you out of the improbable
Future; if you share with all you meet your poverty
                                as if it were love;

If you stand among the desert plants—
                the yukka, the spinifex, the cactus, the oak—
   Where the soil is bankrupt and the rains all spent,
Where memory, like money, is a river run dry;
                        if you can trust in what is difficult,

As hard as drought and doubt and hope
                to hold, your lost self and all you have
   Survived your only angels; if you can gamble with that gift
Which is only yours to lose—
                then you may set flowers

Under the full white moon
                       or you will, if it pleases you, surrender, by day,
  Fragrances sweeter to the air than apples
To the fall and grasses to the spring.
                              You will thrive, in truth,

Only where you think you can't.
               Only in the future
  You cannot see, only in the present
That almost eludes you, will your feet find you,
                                     and stand you in your life
                                         and walk you home.

A Morning

AND WHAT THE FUCK is this day for? I ask,
    Another godforsaken, glorious
            Dawning, as I lie and look at it
    From the bed where I've woken
            Broken again by the weight sleep makes me
Bear and offers me no help to hold. In sleep I lose
    My feet; by night I lose the ground
  I make up in the light, and mornings give
            Me no place fit to stand. This day
                    Waist deep in May—

        The autumn sun spring's fraud
Daubed upon the claret ash,
                    The ornamental maple—
        Shines with an auburn light I know shines on in me,
            Though I am too often dark to it these days.
I know the morning wakes for those I love,
    For the children, in particular, I cannot find
  Or seem to keep, no matter how I try.
                And I know the morning is
                    For them, and because it is

     For them, it is for me,
And it is my life rebooting.
         Like the word in the beginning
     It is god, as they are gods,
        My little ones, and what they want is living.
What the day is for is what my children want
      From me. A love that holds. The only father
   They will ever get to have. To be a light
        For them, to fight a fight for them
          They cannot fight, themselves.

     My body is as slender
As my hope. But hope,
        With all its feathers, is a false
   Prophet when it stands on sands
        Of sentiment. A father must be strong as day,
His life a stay against a child's sorrow and confusion.
      The day out there, I see, is older in its solitude
   Than it ever will be long. And infinite
        Enough to hold a future I cannot see
         Coming, which is parked,

       In it already, miraculous
And murderous at once.
               And just then, my brother rings.
       A friend whose love for me
               Tells me I am worthy of at least another day.
And he stands in the wilderness of grief, the scent
          Of the lover he has lost, not lost in the fabric
     Of a tee-shirt she's returned to him
               Unwashed, like all they knew together.
                  And my love rings then,

       To say she woke foundered,
Sounded and safe
              from a dream of a father
      Who once drowned at sea.
               She's wanted on the earth again, and held by arms
That couldn't save himself, but save her, I say to her, daily
       From sinking too deep below her Self. A knock
   Brings a box to my door and in it
               A tee-shirt I'd ordered for my little girl,
                 Smelling only yet

                    Of manufacture and all
The promise that lies ahead. On the shirt is a meme
                    She loves, a gutsy cat, no cat-gut yet—
          But if she were, she'd be,
                    Like my girl, my friend, my love, and me, the lyre's
Strings, on which all that wants to live would play,
          And all the justice that wants doing
     Would be, like mischief, done.
                    And then a call comes in,
                         The UNHCR,

          Wanting my help with refugees,
But all I have, I tell the man,
                    Is poetry this morning. Call back
          I ask him, when I've saved the little parish of my selves.
                    Then an email lands, selling me the smartest
Shoes a man could ever hope to walk in. Single monks
     In alligator skin. And nothing one can
          Hope to afford. Wisdom speaks
                         In synchrony and counterpoint. The day clouds,
                    Then, the shadow-side

                    Of tenderness, a call
To darker work that love
                            Wants doing for all our sakes. Sometimes
                    The present moment weighs, it seems, too much
                            To lift. But if it's heavy, it's heavy
With better days, freighted also with loss, you'll
            Manifest only by doing the lifting.
    Buckle your shoes, pull on your shirt,
                            Sweat with love's labour, much of it too
                            Hard, that divines the days
                                        To come.

Grief's Work

THE WORK OF grief's the hardest work we get
 To do.
   It is ten thousand miles to go.
It will not stop until we reach the end
  Of letting slide back to the place where it
Began, the love, the life, we knew would never
  End, which ended, anyway, as all
We love will tend to do.
     At every turn,
  Grief runs us off the very road it makes
Us take—deep into the life without.
  I miss like all the days there ever were
The girl who promised all the days to come.
  I miss the children for whose lives I'd give
Up all my own.
     Hope's the only harder
  Work I know. The stars in sorrow's sky.

The Blue Pasture

THE SKY IS a pasture of cloud the morning sun
    Grazes on, and rain is in the offing.

In the meadow, three horses sit and two
    Stand, and so it goes. Most of the work

Is sitting it out, and some is doing the little
    You can. Further along, the Razorback ridge

Is an older and more violent order, reduced
    By time's kind and grinding patience, the way

Things want to go, to this perfection. We're done
    Before we start, but still we start. Three black

Cockatoos, professional mourners walking
    Through their parts, pass low over the winter

Field, and in their wake the morning breaks
    Imperceptibly open. Like any human

Heart learning to love even the loss
    It cannot bear and also the joy that waits.

Two Boys

WHEN YESTERDAY at ten I drove the way
    My GPS—against my better judgment
—Took me, past the house I used to live,
  I saw my two boys walking—the elder now
So tall, the younger still so small—in happy
  Conversation toward their school to catch
A bus.
       And I, their father, bound by law
  And grief and overthinking, could not do
What anyone else who loved them nowhere near
  As much as I, could do: I couldn't either
Stop or toot or wave to them.
                      I smiled
  And drove by weeping, glad of all that binds
Them to each other, glad to see them living
  Well without me, lost in all that keeps
Me from their mornings and stricken in my days.

Three Poems

YOUR soul is seven
    Horses grazing the hillside
In the winter rain.

CHERRY tree in spring
    Rain. Midnight on the road. Time
Overtakes us all.

FROST on paspalum
    Where the heron stalks: winter
At the mountain's feet.

Kite & Cumulus

THE BLACK-shouldered kite
   Sits in laundered robes,
Where she often sits, on
   The wire by the freeway,
Stilled in stolen winter light,
   Prayerful ahead of a kill,
Or replete, perhaps, with
   The morning's after-
Life.
      A few fair-weather
   Cumulus, aping her affect,
Acolytes without a calling,
   Appetites without a parish
Or a prayer, coagulate
   The weeping that the earth,
As if it were one of us, spends
   On each one of us lost.
            And in the Blue-
   Wren blue of late after-
Noon, each cloud, like the kite,
   Looks as light as the spell
The sunshine casts; each
   As still, this day, as sorrow
Is sometimes long; but each cloud
   Rides heaven as heavy
As mourning moves on earth,

    Heavier yet than a passenger
Jet, a stalled and gravid distillate
    Held by the sky as the bird holds
Her breath, quick as the death
    Of her prey.
              Today, as I pass,
The kite shrugs her black
    Shoulders and stays. Like grief,
That broad-daylight thief, she
    Stands and fishes the fields
With her gaze, for as long
    As it takes fresh want to grow
Wings. Making, meantime,
    Light work of the wait.

Come, Play

COME, PLAY with me again, god; come,
    Beloved of the letterbox, play—strip me

Of my sloth and light my eyes with lust
    And dust my loins of loss and ash and fire

Up my fingers for the fun; come,
    Play, sparrow fossicking the gutter

Of the house next-door; come, play,
    Trough Hill, Stonequarry Creek, Wollondilly

Sheoaks, you Sweetgums of the Bargo,
    You potholes of the Mermaid Ponds, come play.

You amber gingko opposite, dressed in the colour
    Of love—I see how you refuse to yield

To winter till it's spring (I'm sure you step
    A foot or two, rehearsing, every night,

This way and that, the moves we don't think you know
    How to make; I know you only seem

To stand exactly where you stood each day
    I wake). Come, all you work that waits—wait,

And play instead with my life; teach me again
    To make my work my play. And come, you passing

Truck; come, you dreams, you re-run traumas
    Of trouble with the spouse, the same old weary

Drama I stepped into at the start—hopeful
    And cocky and blind with kindness, beguiled

By beauty, dumb with desire, sure that what
    Could never turn right would come right

If it would only play my tender and tenacious
    Game of chance. And come, bluewren, make a child

Of me and catch me up in bright elastics
You stretch like plastic chants across the street.

What the Light Tells

MOST OF IT is black, and the beginning goes on
    And on; endings, too, it seems, don't end.
Grief you never do will never stop
    Undoing you. An email from a lover
Whose only home I am, she says, two years
    After I left it. And another love
I've had to shut down, as if one can. And last
    Night, my daughter, her single evening with me
Of each week, won't sit beside me on
    The couch, but listens, where she lies, and laughs
As I read, as if the world my voice makes of
    The book we share were the safest place she knew.
Start over, make a hearth, shape a living
    Constellating all the points of light.
Like your daughter, be braver than you know
    How to be brave.
                Write with your days the lines
That run between the stars. Have faith only
    In the long story that's run from the start.

Picton Morning; Picton Afternoon

For John Foulcher

A NOTHER TRAIN rolls past, metal on metal,
                through the timbered morning
                              light, and tree frogs along the gorge bell the music

  Of the dawning wisdom of all things; they tell you
                      secrets they need your words to hear,
                              they need your life again to lead. Eternity,

All that ever mattered and all that ever will—all
                      the holiness we visit on the gods and wish
                          that we could know—culminates

  Every moment in every moment
                      we nearly always let slip. The life you'd meant
                          to lead gives itself up, abandons

You to yourself, every minute, right here,
                      within your reach, and the sheoaks stand
                          and paint the distance on the sky.

  They wash the future over everything that's past.
                      They spread their arms and ask:
                what's keeping you

From your days? But they know one has to stand
                      sometimes in thresholds longer than one
                          ought, when time is torture and moments

Find it hard to stay. A life has fallen from you;
                        another waits for you to take it
                                      and make it beautiful as a world,

Happy as a child high up in a tree, contented as your lover
                        in the only arms she ever wants. You're wiser, remember,
                                      than you remember how to be. Your fears

Are just a weather that wants to pass.
                        Your sorrow is the world's;
                                      find company in it. Each grief's a friend,

Writes Rumi: ask her in, take her coat, fix her
                        a meal; grow hungry again
                                      and happy in the solace you help her find.

Fall where there seems to be no ground
                        to hold you; find your feet in falling;
                                      let the light carry you the way it did before you came.

Spinebill unspools midday; bronzewing
                        pulls it taut again across the early afternoon.
                        She loves you, calls the butcherbird,

From the ridge of the neighbour's shed—no matter
                        how much faith you think you've lost
                                      in all the beginnings that seemed to end. (She loves you

Not.) From the east, where all things start
                        again, a breeze picks up;
                                      clouds go, freighting sunlight on their backs.

Be borne by what you cannot bear.
>Stop waiting to be over it, in case you never
>>Are. The day is your child. Take her hand. Begin.

My Children Are in My House

MY CHILDREN are in my house again,
    And my heart should be at its ease.
     She asks me if I can braid, and I say
  I'll try, and upstairs she hands me
A brush, and I make two sloppy slender
    Ropes of the silken flax she has for hair.
     Confused and delighted, as I am, at this
    Intimacy she has missed—a father's hands,
Awkward with masculinity and want
   Of practice—my daughter forces a smile
    For a photograph I feel like a paparazzi
  Taking, as if the moment weren't enough,
And undoes them—*imperfect!*—and asks me
  To help her make other arrangements.
                           I've prayed
    For these small domesticities, and
  She has, too, I think, these four long
Fractured years, and we're up for
  Them now they've come, but unused,
    Fingers clumsy and faces mechanical,
  Hearts like plovers finding home.
                      My son,
Gone on gifts I've given him—Arrow,
  And Flash and Lantern and Adventure
    Money and small change—
  Thinks he catches me call this

Superhero thing a phase, and he
   Tells me, no, it will never end.

    Something is here among us; something
  Is not. An absence, singular as
My middle boy, who's stolen himself
   Away. We are a phrase resumed, which
     We had all thought endless, and which,
  Leaving a marriage,
                   I broke. I want that
Ease I knew with them; they seek it,
   Too. But faced with it, and time that runs
    ·Away too fast, we baffle and baulk, and the house—
   Where my children spend an afternoon
And share this one meal with me a week—
   Is a tide neither in nor out, and we are three
     Sandpipers, finical in the neap, and the home
   We knew once is loud about us, and we fish
In this tideline for a way we lost.
                     Each small
  Thing is, for a time, too freighted
    With significance to settle into. Let this be
  Enough, then: my children are in
My house again, and they will be here
                     again.

Passing Picton

For Major Jackson

1.

I WAKE from a dream,
   My three children sketched,
Each in a single stroke,
   Taller than they are and thin
As Giacometti figures, drawn,
   Each a single arc in a coloured
Pencil, my girl in scarlet, my
   Elder boy in orange,
The middle boy in blue,
   And first my girl and then
Her brother, who were with me
   Yesterday, erased, and I know
There is a worse grief than the one
   I feel for them alive, and I know
My lesser grief, and theirs, is grief
   We can survive.
                I lie in bed,
Tears coming hard now, and I call
   Out like the child I am in my
Sadness: No.
            But some joy finds me
   Too: that in the waking
World, though they are hardly ever
   With me, and may start to
Believe I never was, they *are*;

    And wherever they are,
I am.
        I live *in* them, if not *with* them;
    And we have not disappeared.
                              Yesterday
On the balcony, they spoke
   A spate of memory
—*What was the first word I said?*
   She asked me. *Remember what
I said*, he asked, *when you carried
   Me into the room where D.
Had just been born*? And I said
   *Do you remember when you took
Your first step, my boy?*—and all
   Our speaking was a conservation
Of the habitat we are, a talking
   Down of silences in which we
Cease.
      But this,
   Specifically, is the minute or two
Of familial commonplace, I sat just now
   To write:
              When we were on the train—
Only one of them could have
   Spoken this, of course, and
I think it was the boy, but his sister
   Was with him and affirming
With nods, and correcting him,
   As little sisters will,
Saying now, *it was last weekend, H,
   When we went to the city; JP was with
Us, remember*—and my boy rolled his eyes

And carried on—*well, anyway, when*
We were on the train and it stopped at
   Picton—a couple of times, actually, L;
Not just that once—but, anyway,
   We looked out the window and we could
See your place and we saw you
   On your balcony. You did? *Yeah,*
We could see you there.
                     And I wondered,
   As he told me, if they really did.
But they're insistent:
                 Yeah, we saw you.
   I hug them then and find no words
To say.
       It doesn't matter if they
   Saw me; what matters is they looked.
What matters is I was seen, and
   Seeing me, my children, too,

2.

Are seen.
        My children—passing
   With their mother, with their cousin
Down from a hard and humid north;
   My children, stealing a brave look
Sideways; passing, when they knew
   They might have been staying;
Finding themselves wishing, maybe,
   It was still those old and simple days,
When this was a journey
   I'd have been on, too—

My children looked for me,
   And where they looked, I was.
And here on my balcony, I have not
   Disappeared. And, they wished
To tell me, neither had they passed
   From view.

        Yeah, we saw you, my boy says
Again, and my girl nods. And
   I want to tell them: there on that
Train and in your rooms and
   In that watercolour painting your
Perfect life must sometimes seem,
   Among your rabbit and your dog
And your ten thousand pretty things
   To eat and do, you have not disappeared.
We will always see each other
   Even when we can't.
        Our one life,
No matter how much like a train
   Derailed it might feel, its carriages
Uncoupled and fallen down the banks,
   Our one life is a train upon the tracks,
And we take the trip together, and we
   Will not disappear.

3.

        The son of the old couple
Opposite passes by below me in a yellow tee
   And shorts, leading out his parents' dog,
Which they're too old to walk.

                             And in the time
    It's taken me to rise and sit and write,
He returns, and I am still where I was,
    On my balcony, walking circles
In my head, and the dog is exercised
    And tired and the day
Is already long begun.
    Walk your dog, I hear myself say
To myself; take out your life
    And all that dogs it
And steep it in morning light;
    Don't let it lay you up here any
Longer in the past.
                    In their way,
    Yesterday my children
Were saying that, too. Trying to
    Walk their grief out of my head. To
Let me know they know my life
    Without them may be dark—
As blue and grey and shot with silver,
    As four-footed and powerless and
Indefatigable as this midlife cattle dog.
    They feel it, too, the dog of sorrow,
And they know I brought it on them,
    And they begin to know why and
They begin to forgive me, and they want
    These unending days of rending
To begin to end.
                    Yesterday,
    They were consoling all of us
In our single grief.

4.

                Later,
  In the last minutes we knew
We had together till who knows
    When, they hid themselves, my daughter
In the linen press, her brother in the spare
    Room, and I counted to ten and
Called out, *ready or not,* and sure
    Enough, in moments, though they
Thought themselves well hidden,
    I found them where they were.
And so this morning—I school myself
    To hope—it will always be.
                      My lean
    Children, parentheses in my waking—
One of them, then the next, erased,
    An image I'd read as death in sleep
And woken from, crying hard against
    The odds—my children have not
Disappeared. They hold a vision
    Of us and they hold it fast against
The rubbing out each passing
    Day practises on it.
                    Writing this, sitting
On the balcony where they saw me,
    I tell them: *I see you, too.*
                        And whenever
You feel you're passing, or I am
    Written from your book of days,
You will look for me from trains,

    And I will look for you from balconies,
From inside pain, and there we'll be.
    And we, who see without regard
For what they say we can't,
    We will never disappear.

Along the Road

IN THE BOTTLEBRUSH, the wattlebird;   along the road, the rush.
   Blue wrens ring like days undone,   and all I've lost comes home with dusk.
At my desk in silence,   after days in the city, I weep.

Between

THE ELM is leafing out—the first leaves like the last words she said.
Between the rail-line and the road   the garden keeps an old peace.
Between one life and the next   I give thanks for what is, what was.

FOUR ROOMS

IV

First Light

First Cold Night

Everything is plundered, betrayed, sold,
Death's great black wing scrapes the air,
Misery gnaws to the bone.
Why then do we not despair?

—Anna Akhmatova, "Why Then Do We Not Despair?"

THE FIRST COLD NIGHT of the year falls deep
In April, and the base note of finished fires farther
North holds and holds inside the quiet of the air.

The dark so dark it is the earth before the earth
   Began, and in it everything is recollected.
And loss becomes a kind of expectation, grief

A kind of gratitude. Eleven o'clock leans against
   My car and looks back into my house, lit
Where I have left my mind to sit a while

Among its books and schemes and demons.
   Where there are always trains, none pass
Tonight, and all the lazy constellations stall;

Heaven herself has fallen down and felled
   The roses that should be standing by my door.
The new moon has shipped its tender

A GATHERED DISTANCE

Freight of hope beyond the western hills,
    And where my daughter spent a Saturday
Making a mess of my balcony upstairs,

There's still the mess she made; and still
    The mess she made, the glue she spilled,
The flecks of gold, take care of me tonight.

Memory mends me, the broken bowl of me
    The whole of me again, in her hands. And let
Me wear this healing, the scars of our coming

Together again, like learning, lightly
    In the thoughtless kindness of the night.
My cat, Sappho, calmer kin of that poet

Of the broken heart, looks out from the window,
    Her eyes wide with wondering what the hell,
But I stand a little longer in the first cold night

Of the year, for this is emptiness out here,
    And it will fill again in sleep, but while it holds
It holds me, too, and the world is still gassed and

Gas-lit, hacked and swindled and deceived, and I
    Am, too, but the night is void of this for now,
And all there is is all the love one's life is worthy of.

Slime Rhymes

I KNOW A THING that stretches far and makes a rhyme with time:
　　Composed of things that don't belong, the inner life of crime.

　　As prisons go, it's not a jail you'd ever hope to break.
　If freedom one day wanted form, here's the form it'd take.

It's like the love I have for you, which doesn't know an end.
　　The neatest mess two hands can make; a mess the years will mend.

Back When

B ACK WHEN it used to rain,
              there'd be clouds across
   A night like this. But the sky is taut with mourning
So deep no tears will start.
                    I, though, weep for my children—

They and I a semi-fortified
                 encampment ransacked one day
   In late July a year or two ago. Love's work now
Is five parts hanging in there, and four parts
                              letting go. Waiting

Out the fracture. Sweeping up the mess.
               Backfilling every rift, meantime,
   With awe. Keeping faith in silence. Hymning,
Where you find yourself, a hearth,
                       and sitting by it

Till it burns. The future wears a blindfold,
              and it walks the other way.
   But all things pass, like pilgrims,
Each moment hungry for the next,
                   the ground of being charged

With change. Each wound you feel
                an orphan at your door. Rise and let
    The outside come back in. The hills, for instance,
Stand around tonight and speak of us
                                and burn slow, coming

Into endless old beginning
                again; and they find your voice
    And cry your children's names. The night holds
The space wide open, and soon
                        tomorrow's rain will start to fall.

Picton Clouds

PICTON CLOUDS after seven days of sun.
   Rain withheld all winter wants to come,
But still at nine the sky is holding fast.
   Last night I spoke of Vincent to my girl—
Is he the one who did the Starry Night?—
   Of how the gift of seeing deep and other-
Wise can cost you half your mind. She,
   Whose mind is fighting like a fish on a line
To free herself to be herself and love
   What and how she will, nodded and said:
Stop crying or get out of the car.
                        Today the sky
   That draws these hills up from their well is all
She wished she could begin to understand—
   A Van Gogh canvas the Establishment
And all the arbiters of all that's right
   Will try till evening to paint out.
                        A rage
Of tender light burns back the edges of
   The massing clouds, a blue that plain refuses
To grey—the same plangent cerulean
   That looked like madness in the artist's eye.
The apples and the ashes on the hillsides
   Darken, and blackberries bunch the grasses like mobs
Of sodden sheep. And two rosellas who nest
   The silkyoaks, which make their amber claims

Into the air beside the vacant lot,
    Wear the unbearable brilliance of the way
Things really are.
                  Finding hope each morning
    Is weary work the birds perform like falling
Light. Sometimes the mind, that fast machine,
    That motor mouth, makes heavy weather
Of the days; sometimes the world, itself,
    Makes a man work hard, his daughter harder,
For the joy that is their duty and their right.
    So: labour in love and make her burden light.
One's own body, a place one rarely spends much time,
    Eroding like the ageing hills, remains
A postcode where anyone else would gladly live.
    Cicadas, quieting in the overcast,
Still sing; they risk their one week's lease on life
    To advertise among the hungry, and all
Who'd rather not attend, their thrilling instinct—
    Ours—for immortality; in viridian
Notes, in flats and sharps, and viols and harps,
    They cast and cast again that *exquisite spell*
Everything else that will not last has made up
    Its mind to break.
                      My son and daughter told me
When we spoke of Vincent's art last night,
    Curators had found in one of his works, stuck
In the impasto of the artist's azure passion
    Transfigured into cloud—curators had found,
Caught between the notes of its sunlit song,
    Stopped in the thick its one small life,

A cicada, preserved, that's almost now extinct.
    And recalling that, I feel the altered breeze
Come in the window and tug my sleeve, and I look
    And see the aubergine shimmer of the trees,
And in the sky the blue reprised, and I hear
    Cicadas swell and bluewrens begin to cant.

A Boy, One Afternoon

WHEN HE WAS YOUNG, I carried him on my chest;
    I jumped with him; I jogged with him, his heart
Reprising mine, one Christmas in the rain.
    A boy of appetites and dreams and frights,

He eased when I breathed with him and spoke
    With him and sang. As he grew, we duelled; like all
The best books and all the best love, we were tender
    And we were tough. Once when he was four, perhaps,

Or five, and didn't know where to put his rage, I took
    It up and put it outside with him and told him
To let me know when it was gone. He stood
    Aghast at the glass and wanted me dead a while,

And I thought he'd never forgive me, and when
    I looked again he was gone—off to petition the stars
And cry the night down in the yard. Twenty
    Minutes later, he tapped the glass, and I let

Him in, and he took himself to bed. At dawn
    I found him sleeping next to me, the whole world
Right again. Years passed, and it was after-
    Noon, and I stood there at his school. Waiting,

Though not for him, for he had learned, those years,
    To forget the songs we'd shared. It was his brother
I waited for, though I feared today he wouldn't
    Come, and I was right, but as I stood,

I watched my boy whose compass I'd been, his north
    Mine, make his way, alone in the sun, sullen
And resolute, one hundred feet from the hall
    To the gate, refusing to see the father he saw.

Knowing his grief, the silent creed he'd been
    Recruited to, I let my child pass.
But all our old words welled in me and yelled
    At me like worlds to go and hoist him high,

And run with him until my name was one
    With him and happy in his chest. The glass
Still stood between us, I saw, and he was still
    Outside, his hand-me-down rage his own for now,

His love in hibernation in his heart. If this were
    Winter he'd wake from it, if this were a dream
It would end. Instead it's a sentence we both have to serve,
    A phrase that fails, a sonnet that wants to turn.

On Bowral Station,
Waiting for the Early Train,
One July Morning

FIVE daffodils stand
   In light winter rain: the old
Words to some new song.

The Leaves

The trees are coming into leaf
Like something almost being said...

—Philip Larkin, "The Trees"

    SPRING HAS dressed the elm in leaf again—
       The same design as last year, by the look
Of things. But everything worth seeing is worth
    Believing twice.   And just when you begin
To feel you've said it all already and left
    The world unmoved, yourself undone, the spate
Begins, the end of things that had seemed set.
    Winter, like despair you wake to every
Day, fools us every year it will not
    Yield, but all things will. Every line
Of every poem, each new sentence, each new
    Phrase.   Every childhood, every ageing
Anguish, every argument you thought
    You'd lost when it began. And every loss,
Too, turns, in its season, into what
    It is this leaving seems to want to say.

First Light

SO IT begins: first white blooms, like first stars
　　At dusk, start low down. Blossoms string the lower

Branches. The rest of the tree—a plum by the hen
　　House, by the vegetable patch where winter seedlings

Start to rise, by the compost heap where loss
　　Becomes new ground—buds too. But you can't see

That yet; the day has not quite come. Each year
　　Spring starts before winter shuts up shop. And these

Six or seven blossoms open like hands, like the faces
　　Of those you've loved, like your own childhood

Days, which tried so hard to please a world that
　　Was not easily pleased, and practised a beauty you

Did not know yet how to feel. You feel it now: it cuts
　　In. Sorrow burning holes in the darkness. First light.

A Star Fell Last Night

For Donna Ward

A STAR fell last night—
   A little patch of heaven's
Ceiling paint—when I stood
   On the stoop, looking up
After dinner, with my friend,
   At that dark commonwealth.
          Eternity, I must tell you,
Remained thoroughly unmoved.
   The milky way, that ten-million
Mile Nile of the sky, that sly
   And vestigial crocodile,
Slid as ever, slowly,
   On its Way.
          And so it is
With the heart, which is dark,
   Too, and fathomless, and
Perpetual until the end, its
   Trails of pilgrimage, its lane-
Ways of desire cobbled
   And strewn with tea-lamps
Laid out by children long after
   They should have been in bed,
And strung with candles always
   Guttering and threatening
To go out.

How hard it is to let
   What's done with pass.
Sorrow and gladness; languor
   And remorse: you think
The difference matters
   Among the stars?
          Still, oblivion looked
A little blacker to me, after
   That small star had ceased,
And just a little closer
   Toward home. And one
Planet up there, a child
   At the grownup's picnic
Of the Southern Cross,
   Burned pinker than I ever saw
A planet burn.
         And I'm not
   Ashamed to tell you I wept
As I stood there in that star's
   Wake. And only the Beloved—
In me, up there, out there—
   Could begin to tell you why.

A Small Poem for Spring

LIFE SEEMS TO ASK too much of those
  Who ask so much of life.
                        It asks
What winter wants of spring—first
  To wait too long and then to break
Too soon and then to call the sun down
  Soft to help life thrive. Or else let
Winter win.
            But winter won't;
  That's not the way the weather rolls.
Gladness is a duty like that which
  Pulls the blossoms out of the depths
Of drought and plays them on the ends
  Of limbs that look as if they've no love left
To give.
        It asks the body to make itself
  A vessel for the soul, which finds no more
Fault with pain than ecstasy, no less delight
  In rain than light, like that which makes
A temple on the carpet here, in which
  The cat, that poet of old words, becomes
A goddess again and lets herself be praised.

Grace, and a Barking Owl

Almost seventy years and nothing has killed me.

—Ellen Bass, "Indigo"

FIFTY YEARS or more, and nothing's killed me—
No, not even the wreck I walked from Friday

On the corner of Fitzroy and the road north. My car
   At the yard after looks the way I'm inclined

To feel. But it pays to take care with metaphor.
   I still run, if not so fast, and my body

Isn't yet beyond repair. Later,
   In shock, and as the night came down, I swept

A long dry winter's harvest from the playground
   At the school, and there I learned a lesson

From the leaves: gentleness will shift
   What no force moves. Later yet, and some

Of daylight's trauma spent and all the leaves
   Unstuck, I watched the moon, one night short

Of full, catch like a balloon in the canopy
   Of grey box, and from somewhere just beyond

The reach of thought that didn't want to stop,
    An owl let fly her plangent cry: lament

And ecstasy at once. One moment, terror;
    Beatitude the next. The way things are

Is everything and what it cost at once.
    I smiled and felt my heart begin to slow:

Form and how it speaks are near enough
    To all the wisdom we will ever know.

Morning came, and with it rain, and peach trees
    Drew their snowstorms up and parked beside

The road. And at the bottom of my yard
    Plum trees stand around like girls you used to

Know. They smoke their Lucky Strikes and act
    As if they don't want you or anyone

To see them in their beauty, which they wear
    But barely know, and rain falls soft as mercy

On the way they've tied their hair. Soon,
    When all that isn't perfect takes a break

From being wrong, you'll feel again, inside,
    The grace your courage looks like in the weather

Of your days, getting on with the
    Resistance like a wagtail in the snow.

Talking Death Down

I WAKE AND rise and talk death down; her case
  Is strong, she makes it hard, but all her case

Is doubt and lies inside my head. Fall
  Passes, the morning clears, the garden's dressed

For Spring. Yesterday, when winds buffeted
  The car, I sat with my daughter and read with her,

Scout and Atticus again. If that's
  Not life, then life's not worth a single phrase.

Life's a battle you've lost before you start,
  But it's not the winning we're here for; we're here to find

The courage to carry on. Turns out, my children
  Love me, though I've made it hard. Their courage

Warrants my life in return. Joy comes. I tell
  The morning this, and morning carries on.

A Forest Inside

After Kabir

                THERE IS a forest inside;
                        There is a garden and a window
      That opens on it. And there's a bluewren
Wishing the window away most mornings of the world.
        There is a world in me, and it dawns
                When the world about me dawns.
                      The Beloved
          Wakes in her bed in here,
                            When I wake to the Beloved in hers
                                Out there.
                Until then,
       I am the window the bluewren
                          Tries to force each dawn with her
                                        Nimble encrypted rap.

A Scattering

THESE WERE YEARS that I'd set down to spend with you;
   But we were asked, instead, to live these years without

   The company of the other pieces of our names
That families are—those scatterings, those constellated

Selves.
      In truth it was myself I went without,
   For you lived every day that woke and thought that spoke,

   But I was nowhere love was found. From how my years
Were hollowed out, as if I were a wetland dredged,

I fear I know how your lives floundered, too.
                                          The day
Will come when you can tell me all your eyes say now.

   Hope frays the longer it is asked to wait. But still,
Diminished, it persists.
                          And I am like the wader now,

By whose swamp among the reeds along the creek
   They've posted a new sign: habitat, they say,

   Preserved to house the Latham's Snipe, endangered traveller,
When its peregrinations call it home a while

A GATHERED DISTANCE

From Kyrgyzstan and China and everywhere its mind
    Refuses to land long.
                        But what the sign won't say

    Is how, before they drained the flats to civilize
    The suburb's edges more, the wetlands were a vaster

Realm where snipes put down in throngs. Of all there was—
    These easement meters all that holds.
                        And few birds come,

    And so it is with me. But how is it with you?
    We have our wings, our prayers. We have the world, and time.

Today we ride beside the waters, dark beneath
    The winter light—blue and uncertain as your eyes—

    A rare accompanied day among the relic years:
    This tame sequestered chain of ponds—a fallow stream—

Looks just about enough to home our coming back
    To where we never left, this circle of our selves.

The Fire & the River
& the City & the Bush

A MORNING in the city is a couple of packs a day:
                fires ring the Big Smoke, a habit heaven finds it hard as hell
To break, and clouds won't break and rain won't fall, but ash falls
On dinner with your daughter *en plein air*.
                      A consumptive bling on everything urbane.

The air is an apocalypse, an afterlife of trees.
                Contemn the weather long enough, and this
Is what you'll earn: the light, a sallow holiness of grief. Sunsets so
Overpromise in a drought; each day
                    at six a fuchsia bauble decorates the west,

And the beauty daylight dies in
                makes a mockery of hope. El Nino's an affliction
Of the spirit, and every climate crisis starts at home. Want's an empty bucket
At the bottom of a well. Drink
                the earth under the table, and watch the rain

Forget to fall, the rivers how to fill, the fires
                abate, the birds to breathe. But still life refuses to sputter
Or duty cease. And so, you walk from the train at midnight,
And the moon's a blood orange pared on a bench,
                    and who among you ate the other half?

A GATHERED DISTANCE

As if the carpark were a fireground,
                       leaves lie smoked and cured and curled and uncared for,
  As you walk to the car: the spirits of small household gods flown
And fallen here beneath your tired feet,
                       the bodies of the children of Pompeii.

Nights in fire weather are so often
                       like the sea, the days their wreck. All week treading water
  In the pall, while forests fall and rare things fail, you find your way
To the river, at last. But when you find it, the river's hardly there at all.
                       Still, with your children, lucky in their company,

You row. You paddle the downed stream,
                       learning drought in hired boats—an obdurate
  Idiom—all consonants, no vowels—you're asked to master in an afternoon,
When love, itself, takes lifetimes.
                       Nothing's where it should be, but here

You are. Were there no drought, three meters of
                       the river wouldn't fill the city's baths,
  And the river wouldn't run again so close to roughly where it used
To run. (Nothing seems to teach us
                       how to leave it well alone.)

These should be riveroaks you navigate,
                       not stumps. And the waters should yield
  Kingfishers something more to feed their young. Your oars are bargepoles,
And the river is a swamp. But two hours
                       with your children are an ocean when time has been so deep

In drought. This is a paradise you row,
                        lost like the world, thriving on necessity because the future's
  Run so dry. Later there are milkshakes, and soon the day is done. At night
The world burns on. Its boat is beached, but love
                       may come, and with love, rain, and with rain, rivers,
              and with the rivers, brand new words to float the world.

Yesterday's Poem

I SIT at the window working yesterday's poem
Into today's shape, looking out on soft rain
And the grey wind among the water poplars.

FIRST LIGHT

Epilogue

EPILOGUE

Egret in a Ploughed Field

AT THE CLOSE of day, I watch an egret
                            touch down in a ploughed field and earth
   The shallow sky. The ground is scoured where she falls, a soul
Turned, like a pocket, inside out, and the bird wanders
                the black rows, scoring them loosely with its one bright note.

She makes an inverse music, it seems to me,
                            plucking the furrows
   For what they may yield, an improvised notation
That erases itself writing itself down, singing the earth back silently
                                into the belly of a bird, a reverie

In negative, which wakes the dawning dark
                            all the way back to its beginning again.
   The bird's random waltz down unwalled streets goes on—this little
Night music, these white field notes that pull up day's ends by the roots
                                and leaf out the night—

Until the darker music, furloughed
                    here by day, swells and the bird fades, swallowed
   By what she'd divined. And she leaves the darkness more luminously dark
Around the hole she cuts in it, flying the blind
                        field back down to the river.

Notes

Notes

"Desuetude"
This is a poem whose title is a word past its useby. What that word means is "the state of having fallen out of use." Desuetude is a charge often laid at poetry's feet—poetry as a way and poetry as a literature—these days. Poetry is, indeed, another world (the one within) and another currency. We'll be done with poetry when we're done with sex or summer or breathing or language or gods. I wrote this poem because it seemed to want to be made, and I wrote it to stay the personal dilapidation that comes when stories throw down their scripts and stalk away. Marriages, for instance—a story in which one had figured as a father and as a good enough man till recently. "Desuetude" arrived, though, because a musician friend posted on Facebook one Friday that "Desuetude" was her new favourite word, and I was captured by the idea of the antiquated coming back into—or never going out of—style.

"Daedalus at Midnight"
I wrote this poem for an anthology, *Metamorphic*, published in 2017 on the 2000th anniversary of the death of the poet Ovid, author of *Metamorphoses*. The brief was to mention one, at least, of the stories Ovid tells in that book, and the story of Daedalus is one. Daedalus was the father of Icarus and the author of the scheme that led to Icarus's death. He was also the maker of the labyrinth and the hunched maker of fine jewelry. My poem employs one of Ovid's favourite schemes, the Virgilian hexameter (six beat lines), though I did not sustain his dactyls.

"A Gathered Distance"
I wrote this poem, the first of a suite of six, for Red Room Poetry, when I was poet in residence (one of three poets) at the Sydney Botanic Gardens in 2016—part of the Red Room's *New Shoots* project. The poem describes the gardens as I came to know them then (through wandering there and listening to the history of the gardens as its curators know it), and as I could see them, at some distance, from an apartment I lived in that year in Kirribilli. You can find (some of) the poem on a plaque in the gardens, near one of Bronwyn Oliver's beautiful sculptures.
a loveliness of limbs: "For Christ plays in ten thousand places,/ lovely in limbs", Gerard Manley Hopkins, "As Kingfishers Catch Fire".
smooks: I'm thinking of the spelling Cook used for rising smoke he observed as he passed up the East Coast, signs of aboriginal fires, of civilisation, of farming.

"The Habit of Wings"
a burlap sack: I have in mind the imagery in Jane Hirshfield's "Burlap Sack"
like a burlap sack of granite: my image also draws on "I must be dumb as a gunnysack of hammers," from James Galvin's "Depending on the Wind".

"Oblivion"
I've dedicated this poem to Kevin Young because it drew inspiration from his poem of the same name, which I first heard in his voice in a New Yorker Poetry Podcast in 2017. It shares much, including Virgilian hexameter and mood, with my poem "Daedalus at Midlife."
Blue in Green: jazz piece by Bill Evans and Miles Davis. I have in mind the recording by Bill Evans, solo piano, 1960.
peaceful piece: "Peace Piece", improvised by Bill Evans and first recorded in 1958.
unmanned by this too much / to bear references Robert Frost's "Directive": "back out of all this now too much for us".

"Running into my Youth"
In this poem, I've strung, as one probably should not, seven sijo together to make a running meditation. The sijo is a Korean form I discovered when I was asked to write some by Dan Disney for a new journal, *Sijo: An International Journal of Poetry and Song*. In its pure form I have written a number since, of which, in this book "Early Summer Sijo," "Along the Road," and "Between" are instances. I've also written a number like this, where I string several together, and I do so with a bow of deep respect and apology to the form, which I am manhandling here, even as I honour it and carry it into another century and language.
keep my cries: riffs on "cows keep no cry", in Kevin Young's "Oblivion".
low moan: "only a slave's low moan" in Kevin Young's "Oblivion".

"River Running Shallow"
Grief is proof of love: I have in mind thoughts from Julian Barnes's *Levels of Life*.
the sweet music of your particular heart: "Love allows us to walk/in the sweet music of our particular heart," from Jack Gilbert's "The Great Fires."

"Grief Wears a Body"
rust upon the soul: Samuel Johnson's phrase.

"Four Rooms"
Qionghai is a lake in Xichang, by which I stayed with poets from around the world, when I took part in the Xichang Silk Road International Poetry Festival in late 2018. I thank Jidi Majia for his invitation and Jodie Williams for her company. "Hai" in Chinese means "sea" (and "qiong," I believe, "poor"). So the lake is, in the Chinese, an almost, or a wannabe, sea. Langshan is the mountain that rises behind the lake. The hotel where we stayed was roamed by peacocks.
Spring, they tell you, winters here all year: Xichang in Sichuan Province, where the climate is temperate and the mountains high, is said (by the locals, and by Marco Polo) to be the land of eternal spring.

NOTES

"Tomorrow"
This was one of a dozen poems I wrote for the Garden of the Future in Bendigo, a project of TCL. I was creative in residence with TCL through 2017.
trust in what is difficult: Rainer Maria Rilke, *Letters to the Young Poet*.

"A Morning"
miraculous and murderous references Seamus Heaney's phrase in his Nobel Acceptance speech: "a reckoning both marvelous and murderous."

"Kite & Cumulus"
heavier yet than a passenger / Jet: James Richardson, "An Essay on Clouds," *The New Yorker*, 2 February 2015.

"Picton Morning; Picton Afternoon"
eternity culminates every moment in every moment: I'm riffing on words of Ralph Waldo Emerson's in "Self Reliance," where he deploys an old French truism: "God works in moments."

"My Children Are in My House"
we are three / Sandpipers, finical in the neap references Elizabeth Bishop's "The Sandpiper": "He runs, he runs to the south, finical, awkward, / in a state of controlled panic, a student of Blake".

"Passing Picton"
This poem plays with a refrain "I have not disappeared" from "On Disappearing" by Major Jackson. Thank you, brother. You teach us how to see with a just and kindly gaze.

"Back When"
A semi-fortified / encampment: "Tredinnick", an old Cornish name, is said to mean "a semi-fortified encampment" (a gypsy camp perhaps).
Backfilling every rift, meantime, with awe: I'm riffing on a phrase of John Keats in a letter to Percy Shelley, August 16th, 1820: "load every rift of your subject with ore."
The outside coming in; each moment hungry for the next; a slow burning / Coming into endless beginning again: David Hinton, *Hunger Mountain* (p4): "Sincere, generative, hunger-driven—this is what the ancient Chinese understood to be the nature of our Cosmos…Wisdom for them meant belonging deeply to that cosmology of restless hunger…"
I owe this poem to my son Henry, who said, one night, leaving Picton: "Back when it used to rain…"

"Picton Clouds"
exquisite spell: Emily Dickinson: "Life is a spell so exquisite everything conspires to break it."
Apart from that, the poem reports a telling my children made to me of a documentary they watched in which the finding of the cicada was reported. And it records an episode of Doctor Who, in which the Doctor time travels and shows Vincent how the world now regards his work.

www.ingramcontent.com/pod-product-compliance
Lightning Source LLC
Chambersburg PA
CBHW060500010526
44118CB00018B/2479